Thinking About College

MAKING THE RIGHT
COLLEGE CHOICE
TECHNICAL, 2-YEAR, 4-YEAR

Annalise Silivanch

ROSEN
PUBLISHING®

New York

For Rich, and also for Maureen Cunningham, my sixth-grade teacher, because she asked

Published in 2010 by The Rosen Publishing Group, Inc.
29 East 21st Street, New York, NY 10010

Library of Congress Cataloging-in-Publication Data

Silivanch, Annalise.
Making the right college choice: technical, 2-year, 4-year / Annalise Silivanch.—
1st ed.
    p. cm.—(Thinking about college)
Includes bibliographical references and index.
ISBN 978-1-4358-3598-6 (library binding)
ISBN 978-1-4358-8508-0 (pbk)
ISBN 978-1-4358-8509-7 (6 pack)
1. College choice—United States. I. Title.
LB2350.5.S47 2010
378.1'61—dc22

2009021848

Manufactured in Malaysia

CPSIA Compliance Information: Batch #TWW10YA: For Further Information contact Rosen Publishing, New York, New York at 1-800-237-9932

Contents

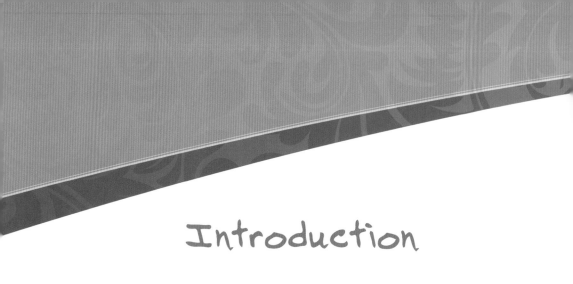

Introduction

Choosing whether or not to attend college is likely the biggest decision you will face during high school. This decision takes energy, time, thought, and intuition. But congratulations: You are taking the time to ask yourself, "What is my next step?" By looking more closely at all of the choices available to you, you are more likely to make the right decision.

And what is the right decision for you? This book is intended to help you discover that. High schools will tell you that college is important for your future, but any college-bound student needs to prepare for this new challenge by spending time thinking about this big decision.

You might be at the very beginning of the college application process, or you might need to make a decision soon. With college costs spiraling upward and many families stretched to afford the basics, it can be hard to separate what you want from what is best for your family. If you struggle with these issues, you'll want to look at all of your options and keep an open mind to possibilities you might not have considered yet.

So before filling out your college applications or browsing another campus Web site, take some time to explore the college decision for yourself. You might discover some things you never realized. Maybe you will glimpse where you want life to take you.

It is easy to feel overwhelmed when you are trying to find the right college for you. However, your needs and interests can lead the way in your search.

Chapter 1

College: Is It Right for You?

"Narrowing down schools was pretty hard for me. I didn't know where I wanted to go or exactly what I wanted to do." —Theresa

"I wish I had put more thought [into the decision-making process]. If I knew then what I know now, I definitely would have taken a closer look at programs rather than money." —Marney

When you think about your life after high school, where do you picture yourself? Are you strolling with new friends on the way to a college dining hall? Are you talking about a new class with a library study group? Are you joining clubs, playing sports, and otherwise settling into your new college home?

Many students feel thrilled about the chance to spread their wings during college. After four years, high school can seem long and even tedious. You may feel ready to meet new people, become self-reliant, and forge a stronger identity for yourself. In your excitement, you can paint a rosy picture of college life. At the same time, new college students find college life full of unexpected challenges. You may be surprised by the intense study sessions and deadlines, roommate challenges, and the difficulty of balancing classes, work, and a social life.

After a long high school career, you may be looking forward to the new friendships and fresh perspectives that college can bring.

You may also find that your college dreams are coming up against the cold reality of finances. Maybe you and your family are unable to cover the costs of full-time college attendance at this time. If you are eager to go, this news can be incredibly hard to manage. The good news is: There are different paths to the same dream, and you still have choices that will get you there.

What Are the Advantages of College?

When you imagine your adult life unfolding, you may envision a great career and independence, but you may not exactly picture your ultimate dream job. The fact is, you don't need to know

College graduates have a leg up on nongraduates in job competition, future earnings, and career options, according to studies.

what you are going to do for the rest of your life. Given the economic changes in the world today, the job landscape is changing all the time. College is not only for those who know exactly what they want to do with their lives, but also for those who are eager to find out.

Labor statistics show there is a financial advantage to receiving a college diploma. U.S. Census data from 2006 found that, on average, adults with a bachelor's degree earned about $20,000 more in annual income than adults with just a high school diploma. The more advanced the degree, the more money you will make. Even a student earning an associate's degree sees approximately a 33 percent increase in weekly earnings.

Moving into the future job market, your degree can impact the range of job choices open to you. The U.S. Bureau of Labor Statistics projects that before 2014, 78 percent of all job openings will require people with some training or education beyond high school. You may still be able to clinch a job by leveraging work experience, but first you need to get your foot in the door. Without a degree beyond high school, it will be harder to get the interviews you desire. Sometimes, that first hire, or that big promotion, hinges on your degree.

Since income affects every part of your life, your level of schooling impacts where you can afford to live and what kind of luxuries you enjoy. Your job category can also give you more (or less) control over your work-life balance, or your ability to make time for your family and yourself. You may already have a job. If you are lucky, it may even be a well-paying job. But ask yourself: Is it the kind of job that would allow me to live as a self-sufficient adult? Is there an opportunity to advance with a high school diploma? Will I be proud to have this job when I am older?

Imagine Your Future

Close your eyes and imagine yourself ten years from now. Then ask yourself these questions:

- What kind of job do you have? Do you work for a big company? A nonprofit organization? Are you self-employed?
- Where do you live?
- What do you do for fun?
- What is your typical day like?
- Do you have children or plan to?
- Can you imagine your final career goal?
- Do you need a college degree to get you there?

As the job market ebbs and flows, a college degree can help position you for the next wave of economic opportunity. Historical trends indicate that college enrollment rises during economic recessions and levels off during periods of job growth. With the right information about financial assistance, such as the aid provided by new government programs, you may find greater access to college than you expect.

Even if you don't plan to use your college degree immediately, the extra schooling will give you more options down the road. You may be thankful to have greater control over your choices. That in and of itself can be worth it.

The Personal and Social Edge

High school students eagerly await graduation so that they can spread their wings in a new direction, and college provides a unique opportunity to grow. In college, you have more freedom to design your academic program, so you can explore different classes and creative projects in a more flexible way. In regard to your career goals, this may help point you toward an area in which you have a natural talent and interest. There is the saying: "If you love what you do, you will never work a day in your life." Why not make your life this fun?

A higher education curriculum allows you to connect with your talents by giving you time to explore the topics that inspire you.

In college, you'll develop skills that go above and beyond the specific subjects you study. Skills such as writing, public speaking, and critical thinking begin before college, but you can hone them much more finely there. Modern careers require people to communicate more rapidly and more frequently, both in writing and verbally. Our ability to communicate affects how others perceive us and receive our ideas. As a result, strengthening these skills can significantly help one's career. Likewise, college equips us to continue learning and thinking critically, digging beneath the surface of issues and making new discoveries.

In addition, you will make connections in college that can be valuable to your personal and professional pursuits. Some of these new friends will be your friends for life. Friends can also help your future job prospects, since social connections are their own valuable resource. Researchers writing in the journal *Career Development International* found that, in the twenty-first century, career success will be increasingly dependent upon the personal and professional relationships that you secure during your schooling, career, and personal life.

Ultimately, college can increase your overall happiness by introducing you to a range of people and experiences that you might not find elsewhere. From exposure to the arts and philosophy, to an increased opportunity to meet new friends and explore new interests, college can help start you on the path to a full and fulfilling life.

Take the Next Step at Your Own Pace

When you think about your life after high school, in what new environment do you picture yourself growing into the adult that you want to be? Do you have the ability to attend college full-time? Do you need to work full-time or part-time as you begin college classes? Are you struggling with the idea that you need to attend college at all? Do you desire one of these things, but fear that the realistic picture is something different? In this chapter, we'll look at some of the options for reaching your goals.

There is no race to a college degree. Even during college, you will find that some of your friends take extra time to finish their courses. High school may be the last time that you find yourself in sync with your peers. You may choose to transition to your next step in a more gradual way, working and taking one class at a time. The important thing is that you commit to beginning your college career and seeing it through.

Some students decide to take a year off before beginning college. After accepting you, most colleges allow you to defer (or delay) your enrollment for up to one year; you can start in the spring semester, or wait until the following fall. If you choose to work for a year, volunteer, travel, or delay starting college for another reason, you still can—and should—complete the application process on schedule. It will be more challenging to complete the process once you are away from high school and your work or personal life begins to take center stage.

The "Gap Year"

In European countries, and increasingly in the United States, high school students take a break between high school and college known as a "gap year." A gap year is a year between high school and college (and sometimes during college) that is spent working, traveling, or in some other pursuit. Harvard University's admissions department strongly advises applicants to consider taking a year off between high school and college. "Such a 'time out' can take many forms," it advises. "It can be very brief or last for a year or more. It can be structured or unstructured, and directed toward career, academic or purely personal pursuits. Most fundamentally, it is a time to step back and reflect, to gain perspective on personal values and goals, or to gain needed life experience in a setting separate from and independent of one's accustomed pressures and expectations." One study found that students showed increased confidence, independence, and "career maturity," or the ability to make decisions relevant to one's career, in the years following a gap year experience.

Some gap year programs are unpaid (and actually cost you money), but there are also many opportunities to find paid work. A number of jobs allow you to live in another state or country and earn money: youth camp instructing, sports coaching, teaching abroad, farming, and working in hotel or cruise ship positions are some examples. Job placement agencies or gap year organizations can help you find a position and advise you about what to expect. In the meantime, do your own research to see what activities interest you and where you might like to travel.

If you want a little adventure before starting college, "gap year" work or volunteer opportunities can bring you to another state or country.

Other students choose to participate in service projects in the United States or abroad through organizations like AmeriCorps or the Peace Corps. While you are not paid a salary, volunteer organizations typically offer a small stipend to cover the necessities.

Depending on the amount of time you volunteer, your service can also qualify you for tuition reimbursement or loan forgiveness in the future.

Other Post–High School Options

If you decide to delay college enrollment to spend time working close to home, consider using the work opportunity to stay productive in other ways. You can spend a year working at the entry level in a field of interest. Before college became so commonly required for many professional jobs, many young people would begin "at the bottom rung" of their chosen career field—literally, in the mailroom or as a secretary. Handling correspondence and other routine duties might appear boring but in fact is a chance to meet people in the field and learn about the typical workday. You may also make the connections necessary to get a higher-level job once you have your college degree in hand. Spend the time getting to know people in the organization. Gather business cards and go the extra mile for people. Once you leave, set up an account on a professional networking site such as LinkedIn. com and keep track of these contacts. When you graduate, they may be able to help you set up the right job interviews.

   If you want to get paid to try something new, consider spending the year learning a trade. For a salary, you might have the chance to learn carpentry, plumbing, construction, or another craft. Writer and motorcycle repairman Matthew B. Crawford suggests that learning a trade can help you hone your self-confidence and skills of attention and observation. "The trades suffer from low prestige, and I believe this is based on a simple mistake," he writes in the *New York Times*. "Because the work is dirty, many people assume it is also stupid. This is not my experience." In fact, you may learn to solve problems in a new way, and these skills will stay with you throughout your life.

Your own community may offer you the opportunity to learn a trade while earning money toward your studies.

The Community College Option

If you are working close to home, you might want to consider taking a class or two at your local community college. By taking a single class or two, you are introduced to college-level study. You may also decide to increase your course load and complete your associate's degree. This degree, typically achieved by two years of full-time coursework, includes many core, or required, college courses. As a result, if you decide to transfer, you can move on to courses in your major at your four-year school. The bonus: If you spend your community college years earning additional money,

Community colleges can help you adjust to college-level academic work and meet new people at the same time. In 2007, 46 percent of all U.S. college students were enrolled at community colleges.

you might be able to head off to your four-year college of choice with a nice amount of earnings saved.

The modern community college is an excellent place for you to find your footing in college-level courses and grow your confidence. "It eases a person into the process of college because it is personal, it was easy to get to know the professors, and I didn't feel it to be intimidating," says Andrea, who plans to transfer to a four-year institution. In 2007, 46 percent of all U.S. college students were enrolled at community colleges.

Classes at a community college can be just as challenging as those at a four-year college. In fact, the list of famous people who attended community college includes a NASA astronaut, a Pulitzer Prize–winning poet, a state supreme court justice, the CEO of Costco, and a United Nations ambassador. Many community college students successfully combine work and classes and thus can be models of good time management. You can assume leadership roles earlier than would be possible at a four-year school: community colleges have newspapers, literary magazines, radio stations, and other groups. Taking this early initiative will only enhance the application to your transfer school.

While a sizable percentage of community college students are older adults, studies show that community colleges work for students of all ages. Students who transfer from community colleges to four-year institutions achieve consistently higher grades than students who begin at four-year colleges as first-year students. Some transfer students report a better ability to focus on classes. Besides, your bachelor's degree will still be from the four-year college of your choice, not from your community college.

Technical School: An Alternative to College

Two-year and four-year colleges fall under the category of higher education. Other trade training programs are known as vocational training, also called vo-tech. Vo-tech programs prepare students for careers in construction trades, such as plumbing, electrical work, and carpentry, automotive repair, culinary arts, medical technology, green jobs, and more. While most high schools offer some vo-tech training, if you want to pursue a technical career, you should plan to enroll in higher-level training within a vocational-technical institute, local community college, or other training center. You can also become an apprentice within the Registered Apprenticeship program of the U.S. Department of Labor. Trainees learn on the job and take classes while working for participating businesses.

Keep in mind that even without college, you'll never be done learning. Vocational careers require repeated training to keep you up to date on the field's most recent advances. The Vocational Information Center (http://www.khake.com) has links to numerous vo-tech schools, as well as information about this education path. Contact individual schools for schedule, tuition, and scholarship information.

Like colleges, vocational-technical schools can be public, private, or for-profit. Given that many vo-tech schools providing certificates of study are for-profit schools, be sure to double-check your prospective school's credentials. The Web site of the U.S.

Vocational programs can help you tap into a passion of yours, such as car customization and repair.

Department of Education provides important consumer information about choosing a career college or technical school, including a list of nationally recognized accrediting agencies. See http://www.ed.gov/students/prep/college/consumerinfo/index.html.

Distance/Online Learning

Distance learning has grown into a kind of partner to traditional colleges in higher education. Increasingly, traditional "brick-and-mortar" colleges are adding online classes to supplement their ground courses. Students who sign up may be anxious to graduate on time or may want a more flexible learning environment because of work or other obligations. Online courses are more likely to be concentrated in their length, allowing students to fit courses into a semester or summer break. There are colleges that are exclusively online, often catering to students who work full-time or have families.

If traditional colleges have not moved entire classes online, they have made their courses more technologically friendly for the "wired generation." Instructors now commonly have a Web site where they can post a course syllabus, assignments, and even host a discussion or question-and-answer forum. Entire online colleges have seen steady growth. In 2006, the Sloan Consortium estimated that the number of students taking online courses increased year-over-year by nearly 40 percent to 3.2 million. Online students, like community college students, fit a slightly different demographic profile than traditional college students: They are generally older, work more hours, and may even have a family.

Online learning presents unique challenges. A student taking online classes needs a strong internal sense of discipline and time management. Virginia's Old Dominion University, which has offered students some kind of television, video, or online-based distance learning program since the mid-1980s, estimates that students need five to fifteen hours or more per week to devote to completing course assignments and activities for each online course, while class discussions may require you to log in at least once daily or more.

If you decide to defer your full-time college career in order to work, find out if your college of interest offers online courses. If you have the time, you can allow yourself to focus deeply on one particular area of coursework and adjust to college-level writing and discussion. You may enjoy the chance to flex your academic muscles.

You may wonder, "How will my course of study translate to online classes?" Your chosen college and major may help determine this. Online learning is occurring most overwhelmingly at the associate's level at public colleges. The most common classes offered online are within the social science, liberal arts, and psychology fields. Notably, colleges with programs from the associate to doctoral levels agree that there is now competition among schools for online students, so the ongoing demand will likely continue to push these programs to improve.

Make a Wise Decision

Have you decided that you'd be happier without college? While this feeling may be perfectly valid, most college counselors would advise you to reflect on what you're feeling. Are you afraid of the completely new environment? If so, consider taking community college courses first to test the waters. Are you feeling burnt-out from high school? Consider taking some productive time off, as mentioned earlier in this chapter. Do you feel that you can't afford it? There are many resources to help break down the cost once you've applied to schools.

You may be surprised at how flexible a college course load can be: In 2002, the U.S. Department of Education found that more than 80 percent of college undergraduates worked while enrolled in college. In fact, a multitude of programs centered on work and service allow students to combine work and school successfully. On your college campus, you may qualify for the Federal Work-Study Program, which connects financially deserving students with part-time employment opportunities. The U.S. Reserve Officer Training Corps program, or ROTC, is a military program that offers college scholarships to qualifying students; you can enroll while in high school or even during college.

You may believe that you can earn decent money without college, now and into the future. Workers with a high school degree may earn a decent salary to start, but their salaries can peak, or max out, earlier in life. You have the best likelihood of earning a higher long-term salary if you choose a specialty and receive training.

If you are still uncertain about attending college or a technical program, you may need to bring your concerns to your high school counselor or a teacher you admire. Find someone to whom you can voice your concerns and fears. Are you not receiving the encouragement that you need? Are you getting all of your questions answered? Are you afraid of the unknown and are just feeling "stuck"?

Social pressures can sometimes play a role in your decision. For various reasons, your family and friends may not fully support your plan to attend school and may pressure you to remain at home and accessible to them, especially if they themselves have not attended college. Despite their good intentions, they may distrust the college environment if they have not experienced it firsthand. An objective yet supportive person can allow you to air your feelings, redirect your intentions, and help you create your best possible future.

Whatever your decision is, make sure you are making it for the right reasons. Make sure the choice is yours and not that of your parents, counselors, and friends. If you don't feel the internal motivation to continue school, ask yourself why. As you enter adulthood and gain additional responsibilities that might include a full-time job and even a family, it becomes harder to return to school. At the same time, not all successful people need to attend college, and there are loads of unsuccessful college graduates.

With any career path, you will need to exercise your motivation and self-discipline to find success. You can create a life without college, but be prepared to get an education! No matter what level of schooling you aim for, today's employees are always students, learning a new technology or training for a new position. Once you discover what you want to learn, the practice of learning and mastering new skills can be a joy at any level.

If you decide that college is still your plan, it's time to narrow down that decision a little bit more.

MYTH: Community college is less expensive, so the teachers must not be as good.

Fact: Community college instructors sometimes have more freedom to focus their time on teaching. It's funding from the state, much more than your tuition, that supports the college.

MYTH: Transferring credits from a two-year school to a four-year school is going to be a nightmare.

Fact: It's easier than ever, especially if you know what four-year school you plan to transfer to and talk to your college counselors.

MYTH: Distance learning is only for techies or slackers.

Fact: Online college courses are carving out a niche in higher education because they can help more students gain access to college. Also, they can be more affordable for colleges to run. While distance learning is not for everyone, disciplined students who are comfortable with this model report high satisfaction.

MYTH: Online classes will keep me isolated from a real learning community.

Fact: Since online classes are generally designed to be facilitative, or to encourage hands-on work and problem solving, you will work closely with your classmates to produce work and share ideas.

Finding the Right School

When you begin to research schools, the process can feel overwhelming. There are more than four thousand public and private colleges and universities in the United States, and some weeks it might seem as if they have all sent you something in the mail. It is easy to get distracted by pretty brochures or become interested in the schools that your friends are talking about. But remember: Your goal is to find a suitable school for you and your plans.

What you may want from a school when you are seventeen can be different from what you want at twenty-two. "When I was eighteen, all I saw was the importance of getting into college so I could put it on Facebook, put a decal on the back of my car, and have my college printed next to my name in the last issue of the student newspaper. That's where my priorities were at the time," says Meredith. As you take a closer look, ask yourself: Will this school allow me room to grow and change? Just as you carefully consider what kind of person you would like to date, all potential colleges deserve a critical eye.

Where can you begin your search? During the first stage of your search, you need to play detective. First, talk to any older high school friends who may have graduated. Speak to a teacher of your favorite subject. In your area of interest, which schools do

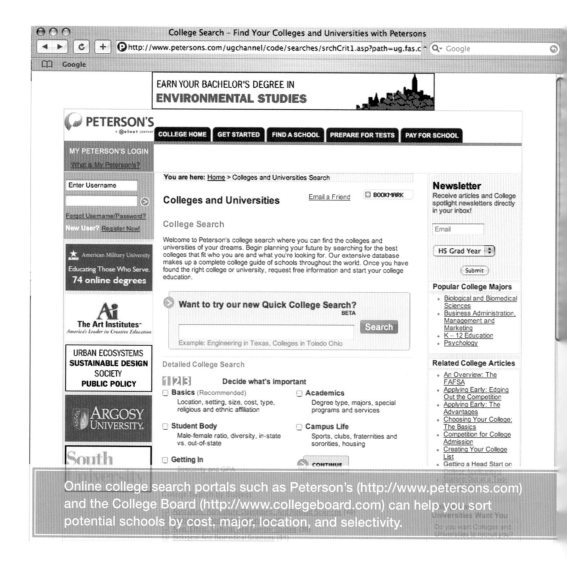

Online college search portals such as Peterson's (http://www.petersons.com) and the College Board (http://www.collegeboard.com) can help you sort potential schools by cost, major, location, and selectivity.

people praise? How does each school promote itself? What values does it seem to emphasize? In which areas of study does it take the most pride—and invest the most resources? It is fun to read lists showing which colleges are ranked higher than others, but that only tells a very small part of the story. Yes, you may be able to trade on the prestige of these colleges later. Also, if their graduates tend to attain prominence in their fields, this can help your

What Is Your College Style?

Quiz yourself. Do you:

1. Thrive with many peers around you? Or do you do better in a smaller setting with more instructor support?
2. Prefer to have a lot of control over the courses you take? Or are you happy trying what the college suggests?
3. Love urban life or imagine yourself in the country? Become happy or gloomy based on the weather?
4. Mind a college with a religious affiliation?
5. Picture yourself at a historically black or women's college?
6. Have a career choice requiring you to take science or technical classes? Liberal arts classes?
7. Want to play sports or be at a campus with active sports teams?
8. Have a special hobby or talent that the school might help nurture?
9. Expect to clinch a great internship? Want to look into a study abroad program?
10. Think you'd like to spend time with laid-back types or highly competitive, professionally oriented students?
11. Want a different level of diversity or political feel than what you experienced growing up?

own networking opportunities down the road. Still, they may not be the best schools to serve your interests, talents, and personality.

Naturally, you'll want to check schools out online or with a book that compiles and compares the most current information on each college. Web sites such as Peterson's, the Princeton Review, and the College Board are great places to begin. On these sites, you can narrow down schools by location, size, academics, cost, selectivity, major subjects, and campus life. One college student calls the College Board site "more addictive than Facebook." Spend some time searching in different ways. It will take some time, but you will find that certain schools will keep popping up. They may be a good fit for you.

Investigating the Programs

If you find a school you like, look at the courses offered in your potential major(s). Adam Gustavson, a New Jersey college instructor with experience at both a private Catholic college and a community college, suggests you look directly at opportunities for advanced study in your area of interest. "Say you want to be an art major specializing in illustration," he says, "but the school only offers Introduction to Illustration in addition to other, very general, art survey courses. Even with the talent, how would you grow your particular skills with only one course?" It benefits a college to offer a wide array of majors in order to promote its wide appeal to students, but that doesn't mean the school will suit your particular needs.

Similarly, Gustavson suggests checking the number of graduation requirements, or classes the school requires you to take in order to graduate. A large number of required courses may mean that your course load has less room for extra courses in your potential major or for other courses of interest. Has the school invested in new equipment for your field, and will you have access to hands-on learning with effective, qualified teachers? Are there

When comparing college programs, determine what criteria are most important. For example, if you thrive on personal interaction with instructors but become shy in a large lecture class, size may be a crucial consideration.

large support programs, such as career and health services, counseling programs, and tutoring services? Ultimately, these resources matter more than how nice your dorm room is going to be.

When you have a short list of schools, you should contact each school to ask more personalized questions. You might wonder: What can they tell me that I can't find out on the Web site? They can answer all of the questions that directly apply to your needs. For instance, if you are black or Latino or in another minority group, you might want to ask about the graduation rates for minorities or if the college has support structures for minority students in place. Also see if anyone knows a student who is enrolled, so you can get some unbiased feedback.

Seeing the Sights

If the school is not far from your hometown, plan a visit with your family. Attend an information session. Be sure to sign in to show your interest and get on the school's mailing list. Take the standard tour, but spend some extra time just wandering around. Check out the interior of the buildings that house classes in your potential major, and ask some students about their experiences. Don't be shy; your family may also be interested to hear other students' opinions. You can ask students questions like: What do they like best about the school? What do they wish they had known before attending? What do they like least? Even if you put them on the spot, they'll surely think of something honest to share.

   If a more distant campus makes visiting impossible, you have alternatives.

A college campus is best seen in person, especially to get a sense of the student population and the feel of the college environment. If you can't get there, a virtual tour might be your next best option.

Web sites like CampusTours (http://www.campustours.com) and eCampusTours (http://www.ecampustours.com) now offer "virtual" tours of college campuses. You won't get the chance to gather on-site opinions through these tours, so you might want to find some other way to do so—for example, through online social networks or alumni associations.

Considering Costs

Your college's likely cost will probably be one of the biggest factors in your decision. The important question of "Can I afford this school?" is worth including in your early evaluations of colleges. Find up-to-date information about tuition at the colleges that you are interested in. You'll also need to delve a little deeper to find out current housing and meal costs, estimated health service and student activity fees, estimated books and materials costs, and any other miscellaneous fees. Calculate this number for each school in order to better make your decision. Consider yourself a customer of this college and ask yourself: Is the money I'll spend at this school a good investment? Is it a reasonably priced investment, or is it astronomical?

If you plan to work during your academic semesters, you might want to find out what jobs are available on campus or in the community. For instance, if you have worked at a store or supermarket, can you find a similar position in your new community? Can the campus provide you with a work-study opportunity, say, in the library or cafeteria? Talk to someone in the student employment office, in the career center, and even at some local businesses to see who's hiring. If you absolutely plan to work, make sure the surrounding area has options for you. In an economically struggling local economy, a high unemployment rate will mean that you'll have a harder time finding a job and meeting your financial needs.

Most of today's college students work during or between semesters to cover costs and have spending money. If you plan to work, make sure that you understand the health of your prospective college town's job market.

Narrowing Down the List

In the end, you will settle on a handful of colleges to which you'll apply. Traditionally, students apply to a highly selective "reach" school; apply to some others to which they are likely to be admitted; and then apply to at least one or two "safeties," or colleges that are certain to accept them. Check with your counselor to make sure that you are not applying to too few or too many schools.

You might want to consider applying to a school whose tuition is a bit higher than you'd planned. If this school becomes your first

Narrowing down your college choices will take time, reflection, and communication with family members. If you and your family are on the same page, each acceptance letter will be a cause for celebration.

choice and you are accepted, you might be inspired to do some serious mining for financial aid. The school may also offer you a generous scholarship or financial aid package if you are an attractive candidate to them.

Of course, your favorite colleges may or may not be the favorites of your family. They may have concerns about the setting or size. Families often prefer colleges that are closer to home and more affordable, like in-state schools. On the other hand, you may be attracted to a school on a distant coast. It is important to communicate openly and honestly with your family so that you can settle on a school that everyone likes. For example, some families don't mind a great separation, but others feel overwhelmed by it. Also, if you attend a distant school, your expected costs will increase because of travel expenses at holidays and breaks. If it is pure independence you are after, you may not need to attend a school across the country. Sometimes, that can be found at the closest state school. If you are open-minded about examining a college that your family likes, you may be able to fulfill both their needs and yours.

On the other hand, you may find yourself "locking horns" with your family on this decision. In this case, take a breath. You may all have perfectly good reasons for your points of view. Now you have an opportunity to gain your family's respect by presenting your side thoughtfully and convincingly. A simple exercise might help clear the air: Take out a piece of paper and draw a line down the middle. On one side, list the advantages of attending the school of your choice. On the other side, list the disadvantages. Do this for each school, making sure that each point is factual, rather than emotional. This gives each person some space to determine: Am I favoring a school for the right reasons? If the negative side outnumbers the positive side for any particular school, it may be a convincing enough reason to strike it from the list.

Families who find themselves completely stalled might want to meet with a high school counselor or another person who can help both sides gain perspective. The meeting may help bring misconceptions to the surface and help you come together in a new way. You might also realize that you were stuck on a particular college for a more emotional reason than you realized.

If you spend the time, you will probably find the right school in the right area of the country, with the right courses, for the right price. In the next chapter, we'll look at the process it takes to get admitted to that "just right" school and how to avoid feeling overwhelmed by this large and important project.

Ten Great Questions
TO ASK A COLLEGE
REPRESENTATIVE

1. What kind of learning philosophy does the college advocate?

2. What percentage of classes are taught by teaching assistants and adjunct instructors? Do professors have office hours for questions and assistance?

3. What course load do faculty carry each year?

4. What percentage of students graduate on time, without paying for additional semesters?

5. Does the school partner with any businesses to offer internship opportunities?

6. How can your school help develop and enhance my particular set of professional interests?

7. How small does a class have to be for it to be cancelled?

8. Do all dorms have resident advisers? What are the official dorm rules?

9. How do I get around town without a car?

10. What makes this school different from the rest?

Tackling the Application

The college application process takes time and effort. A 2008 report by the National Association for College Admission Counseling (NACAC) found that the increasing population of high school graduates is swelling the number of applicants for college. In addition, students are applying to more colleges simultaneously. Despite the work for their admissions departments, colleges actually want—and even recruit for—the extra applications. The more applications a college receives, the more selective it appears. This can move the college up in the rankings and lend it a sense of prestige.

Once you're ready to win over your selected schools, you'll want to create an application that stands out from the competition. But first, let's talk about the basics.

Apply Yourself

Once you compile a small list of schools that seem to suit you and to which you'd like to apply, it might be time to sit down with your family and/or school counselor to get feedback about your plan. Questions to ask might include:

- How likely am I to get into these schools?
- Am I applying to too many schools and can I do the work involved? Too few?

Chapter 4

The College Application Dissected

Application: A form you fill out yourself. This can be in paper form or online.

Application Fee: A fee requested by a college to cover the cost of processing your application.

High school transcript: A form filled out by an official within your high school's guidance office, showing your classes, grades, attendance, and other important information.

Admissions test scores: These are scores from your SAT or ACT.

Letter of recommendation/teacher evaluation form: A description of you and your strengths from a teacher, counselor, or other qualified adult who knows you well.

Essay: Your essay can be autobiographical or on a theme assigned by the college. It is a key chance to express your individuality.

Interview: A personal interview with an admissions officer or an alumnus (graduate of the school). This may or may not be required/recommended by your college.

Portfolio: This is a collection of your best work, required for music, art, or design programs.

- Have I balanced my applications well, with a "reach" school and a "safety" school, and others in between?
- Will I be proud to attend these schools? Will I be satisfied to attend the "safety" school, if need be?
- Do I understand what the applications require?
- What are the application fees and will I have money for those fees by the deadline?

Applying to several schools can be a financial burden for families, but financial waivers for low-income applicants are available. Generally, schools' application fees can run from free to as high as $75. The application fee is usually not refunded, even if you are rejected or choose not to attend. If these fees would pose a burden and your family qualifies as low-income, many college admissions offices will waive the fee. Contact the college's admissions department or ask your high school counselor for a form titled Request for Waiver of College Application Fee. Students who qualify for the College Board's SAT Program fee-waiver service may also be eligible for up to four application fee waivers. Your college of choice may also offer a reduced admissions fee, or no fee at all, if you apply online.

Organizing Deadlines

What is the fastest way to blow your chance to attend your top-choice college? By missing the deadline, of course. College application deadlines are hard and fast, allowing admissions departments the time they need to comb through an enormous pile of applications, essays, and transcripts.

If you are not a naturally organized person, you will need a plan to keep the deadlines for each school visible to you. After all the time you've spent researching the colleges that

Missing just one college application deadline could change your plans in a big way. Develop a tracking system: create a big wall calendar, for instance, or e-mail yourself weekly reminders of what you'd like to accomplish.

are available to you, you should want to carefully plan your application process. For each college, take note of each deadline—for testing, the official application, the housing application, financial aid application, and any additional applications for honors programs or other specialized study programs.

You might ask: How am I going to keep it all straight? Consider an organizational system that works with your natural style. If you are a visual person, you might want to create a separate sheet for each college to post in a place where you can easily see it. As another option, get a large, blank piece of paper and draw a big box for each month of your senior year. Record all of your deadlines, in order, on this sheet. In addition, several of the online college databases mentioned in this book allow you to construct a deadline and task organizer. Some months you'll have a lot to do, and some much less, but at least you'll be able to see it all. Keeping it visible is not intended to stress you out, but empower you to stay on your toes and meet your goals. This system also allows you to break down larger projects, such as writing your college application essay, into weekly or daily steps with some time to relax in between.

If you use a calendar or planner, enter the deadlines there, too. While you are juggling regular schoolwork and activities with college applications, ask yourself: How can I break each application down into daily or weekly steps? Waiting until the last minute can have a negative impact on the quality or accuracy of an application at a time when you want to represent yourself fairly and well. (This strategy is a must when it comes to creating your college essay; we'll discuss this in more detail later in the chapter.)

If you continue to feel overwhelmed by the process, a mentor might be able to help you along. A mentor is someone who acts as a coach for your achievement in your academic or professional life. Such a person can be one of the strongest influences on your success. A mentor can come in many forms: He or she can be an experienced, knowledgeable family member. A mentor can be your high school counselor, if you feel you can get the attention and help that you need. Believe it or not, you can also find a new mentor for yourself. Let's say you want to become an engineer. You might ask your math or science teachers if they know a recent graduate who is studying engineering in college and if they can help you get in touch with the person. You might see if there is a professional engineering organization in or near your community or online. A professional organization consists of many members, all of whom went to different colleges and have opinions of those programs. People in the working world can gather a lot of information for you from coworkers as well. When introducing yourself to a new mentor, it might be wise to have your parents involved in the process, but don't be shy. People are usually flattered to be asked for advice and are happy to help an eager young person.

Early Decision and Early Action

You may have heard of options called early decision and early action. These programs are offered as a chance for you to submit your application by an earlier date. You'll then be judged with a smaller group of applicants. If a college accepts you under an early decision program, you are under an agreement to attend that school. As a result, you can end the application process early, sometimes months before your classmates. Your schools may have an early decision program. But is this a good choice? The truth is, many highly selective colleges have eliminated the program in the last few years, including Princeton

University, Harvard University, and the University of Virginia. Barbara Schneider, an education professor at Michigan State University, found that the competitive nature of early decision programs fueled a kind of "college fever" among high school students. This raised the risk that students would choose a school not well-suited to their interests and needs. Admissions officers also say that the programs favor students who are financially well-off, since an early agreement to attend a college does not give you and your family enough time to determine your full financial aid package.

The Common Application is a single application now accepted by approximately 350 U.S. colleges. It can also help you organize and track the status of your school forms and recommendations.

Unlike early decision, early action allows you to apply early to a school but does not require you to attend the school if accepted. In fact, you can apply to a number of schools as an early action candidate, and you usually have until late spring to decide where you will attend.

The Application

First, make sure you have an application for each school. Today, most colleges offer an application that you can download from the school's Web site, although you can still request a paper copy from the school. If you complete an online application, the school may remove its application fee, since online applications are easier for the admissions department to process. Approximately 350 colleges nationwide now accept an application known as the Common Application (http://www.commonapp.org). Even more schools accept the Universal Application (https://www.universalcollegeapp.com). These services can be a real time-saver if your colleges participate, since they allow you to send the same data to multiple schools.

What information will you need to complete a college application? Many of the sections will simply ask you for basic information about yourself and your family, what term you plan to enroll, possible major(s), and standardized test scores. The application will also ask if you will be applying for need- or merit-based financial aid. Though checking these boxes will not impact your chances of getting into a school, the school will often use this information to send you additional forms.

The second half of the application typically offers space for you to list any academic honors you have received, clubs or activities you have participated in, and work experience. If relevant, work experience can include any extraordinary amounts of time spent helping with a family business or other responsibilities. The Common Application also requires that you divulge any crimes or school disciplinary violations (probation, suspension, expulsion, etc.) you have received and explain the circumstances.

Admissions Tests

You probably know that taking the SAT or ACT is part of the college application process. These tests aim to gauge your math, writing, and critical reading skills to determine if you can approach college-level work. These tests remain contentious. Detractors argue that the tests favor wealthier students and have led to an over-reliance on score-based evaluation. Currently, there are more than eight hundred four-year colleges nationwide for which submission of scores is optional, and your colleges may be among them. If not, you'll need to take an admissions test at least once.

Your first question will likely be: Which test do I take? Quite simply, take the test required by the colleges to which you want to apply. If one or more of the colleges accept either test, you might want to consider taking both and submitting your stronger results. Currently, both tests run around $45, with free online posting of your scores, though additional processing fees (late fee, standby fee, register by phone) may be added. The ACT costs $32 if you are not completing the writing portion. Both testing companies will also charge you more for sending your scores to more than four colleges. Lower-income students may be eligible for a fee waiver. See your high school counselor for more information—and remember that if you apply for an SAT fee waiver, you may also be eligible for a waiver of your college application fees as well.

You can register to take the SAT online at http://www. collegeboard.com (where you can also find practice questions)

or through the mail. ACT registration can be found at http://
www.actstudent.org. Your high school counselor should also
have paper registration forms for both tests. You are permitted
to register for and take both tests as many times as you like.
The College Board, maker of the SAT, recently joined the ACT in
allowing students to report only their highest scores. However,
in order to discourage excessive test-taking, some colleges still
require you to submit the scores from all of your testing dates.

You'll find that preparation will help alleviate the stress surrounding these tests—and help boost your scores. There are

Be Active!

Sometimes, when writing about your extracurricular
activities in your application, the language can make
the difference. Make your word choices "active," rather
than "passive," and highlight your leadership potential
to your college:

Passive	Active
• Responsible for set design	• Designed full set
• Third runner on JV team	• Performed in JV team's top three
• Took pictures	• Photographed
• Got the club funding	• Successfully campaigned for funding

many SAT/ACT prep courses, but you can also prepare for these tests on your own. The Web sites for each test offer specific preparation advice, and your library should carry updated test prep books. Since these tests are used to compare high school students with similar grades and activities, you'll want to stand out from the crowd by taking your test seriously and studying hard for it.

When describing extracurricular activities on your college application, emphasize the initiative, creativity, and leadership skills you used. Above, high school volunteers serve Thanksgiving dinner to seniors in New York.

Activities, Work, and Other Circumstances

No college judges you based on the sheer number of activities in which you were involved. If you list twenty clubs and activities and say that you also worked part-time, admissions officers may wonder: There are only so many hours in the day; how involved could you have been? Rank activities based on

your level of involvement. In other words, emphasize quality instead of quantity. Schools like to see that you participated in an activity several years in a row, with increasing levels of responsibility. The same wisdom applies for any résumé or application: It is not how many seats you warmed, but how active you were in taking leadership roles when opportunities arose.

Colleges are interested to know what jobs you have held, since it gives them an insight into your personal drive and time management skills. A job doesn't need to dazzle them; they know that high school students need money for transportation, time with friends, etc. Still, even the most basic job gives you chances to build your confidence and leadership abilities. See the sidebar "Be Active" for tips on how to present the skills and responsibilities you learned.

Students juggling urgent family responsibilities sometimes find they have had less time to join high school clubs and teams. You may have needed to care for a younger sibling after school or help your parents with a family business. You might worry about this. First, ask yourself if you can include this information under "work experience." If not, the application should have a section for you to explain the responsibilities that have kept you busy. Since the college admissions officers do not know you as a person, it will benefit you to include this information. They simply want to get a clearer picture of your character and motivation. If you rise to the occasion with these personal responsibilities, this could actually impress them.

Recommendations

Do you have a favorite teacher who knows you as a person? If you do, deciding whom you will ask to write a recommendation letter will be easy. If this is not the case for you, you have other options. There might be a coach, school administrator, or community leader who would be happy to provide a letter. The letter should share how the individual knows you and for how long, and what kind of qualities and potential you possess. If you feel you have not worked to your potential in school but have shined in another pursuit, consider asking someone who has witnessed you at your best.

Whomever you choose, feel free to give your letter writers some brief notes detailing your career goals, and how you feel you are growing academically and personally. They might appreciate the extra details to fill out their perspective. Most importantly, be sure to ask them as early as possible. If your recommendations do not arrive in time, the college's decision will be made without this information working in your favor. Worse, your application might be dismissed as incomplete.

The Essay

Of all an application's parts, the essay seems the most mysterious to students. Most everything else is cut-and-dried: these grades,

Your college essay can capture your individual voice and spirit in a way other parts of your application cannot. Give yourself plenty of time to reflect on your essay topic and to make sure the writing represents your best work.

those scores, this letter. But how should you wrap your head around a successful essay, and what tone should you aim for?

Parke Muth, associate dean of admissions at the University of Virginia, tells *USA Today* that having a good essay is not the same

Acing the Essay: Some Tips

The personal essay is a key component of your college application. Writing a strong essay can help move your application to the "yes" pile. The following are some tips:

- Choose an essay topic that highlights an interest, hobby, or talent.
- Expand on—rather than repeat—the information you have listed elsewhere in your application. Write about something interesting that happened in one of your activities.
- Bragging is unnecessary, if not annoying to admissions officers.
- Don't write about discovering the meaning of life while on vacation. Travel essays are the most common submission. Try to find a topic that is unique.
- Don't write to shock or attract attention.
- Be honest without confessing all of your secrets. Just stand up for yourself.
- Imagine that your reader needs to pick you out of a crowd. How would your personality distinguish you? Try to include such details in your essay.
- When writing about your qualities, pick one or two, not all of them.
- Choose a topic that is truly meaningful to you. Write with your head and your heart.

as having strong high school classes and grades, but it can make the difference for some students. Why? Because it is the college's best chance to hear your voice. Here are some essay topics modeled after those most commonly used:

- Reflect on one meaningful achievement, dilemma, experience, or risk you have faced and how it affected you.
- Write about a person who has had a profound influence on you, and why.
- Write about a local, national, or international issue and why it is significant to you.
- Describe an experience that demonstrated the value of diversity to you.

Be sure to read and reread the essay topic so that you understand what you should try to accomplish in your writing. Most likely, you will also have the option of coming up with your own topic. Do this carefully, though. Sometimes, the assigned topics or questions help create a more focused essay, allowing your perspective to come through. Remember, this essay should introduce readers to your unique voice, with all of its qualities and character, so they can envision how you will add to the vibrancy of their college.

Finally, give yourself enough time to take this important piece of writing through all the steps from brainstorming to a final edit. If you write the entire essay the night before the application is due, you lose the chance to ask a friend or teacher to read and comment on it. You lose the option to give a better topic or idea a chance. You lose the time to put your writing down and return later for a cleaner edit or tighter focus. You also lose the certainty that you wrote the best essay of your life.

Application Extras

Are you inspired to add something extra to your application? Be careful when deciding to send supplemental materials. First, don't even consider sending gift items of any kind. This is unethical and will make you appear desperate. If you have not had the chance to showcase a particular artistic talent and believe you would be an asset to the college's program, call the appropriate college department (such as music, dance, etc.) and ask if they would like you to send a video or recording. If they are interested and see your skill as an asset, they may put in a good word for you to the admissions department.

Don't send a video of you on your sports team. If the school's athletic department wants to see you in action, they can contact your high school coach. You also do not need to send extra letters of recommendation, research papers, packets of poetry, or the yearbook you helped photograph. Admissions officers are skilled at their jobs and know what to look for. Focus on creating a great application instead.

Beyond the Fat and Thin Envelopes

The time spent waiting for the colleges' decisions can be stressful. The good news: Once you have sent off the best applications that you can create, the result is out of your hands. This might be a good time to spend extra time with friends and enjoy how your high school career is winding down. When the letters do arrive and you muster the courage to open them, you'll have a better sense of where you will be heading in the fall.

Congratulations!

If you are accepted to one or more of your choices, you'll be breathing a little easier. With more acceptances come more choices for you, of course. This can serve as its own stressor: Now your future is really in your hands.

Whether you are just trying to keep track of one school's acceptance paperwork, or you want to more closely scrutinize several schools that accepted you, a new system of organization will help. A student named Andrea explains, "[After the acceptance], the letters began to arrive as to what documents the school required. As I received them, I kept them in a folder that was easily accessible. I marked down the dates they were due back—actually, I wrote the date to be a week earlier, in case a problem arrived that I

When college decision letters start arriving, you may feel that you're on an emotional roller coaster.

didn't expect. It has been over two months since I received my acceptance letter and I am still receiving mail . . . letting me know of more required documents."

Most important, you'll want to learn what financial aid package each college offers to you, including scholarships, loans and grants, and any money you have sought out yourself. With each aid package, you'll have a sense of what the school will really cost

An Acceptance Checklist

A college's acceptance is great news, and you'll want to celebrate. You may also need to make a tough, final decision if multiple colleges accepted you. Some to-dos during this stage:

1. Send your own acceptance letter so that the school knows you are committed.
2. Officially decline all other college acceptances by phone or letter. The sooner you do this, the sooner a waitlisted student can be accepted.
3. Make sure that you talk with your family to understand how cost, location, course offerings, and other factors make your first choice the best choice.
4. Complete this correspondence in a timely manner, without any rash decisions.

you and your family. At this point, you and your family will want to sit down again and evaluate the costs. Which school has come to the front of the pack? Can everyone agree, and for the same reasons? Can you begin at the traditional fall start of classes? Are you postponing or deferring? This discussion is crucial, since you'll need to make sure that you and your family can manage the true, just-around-the-corner costs of college.

When a rejection comes, it can sting. Instead of stewing in disappointment too long, talk it over with friends, family, and maybe even your high school counselor. A college's decision is not a personal critique.

Rejected? Waitlisted? What Next?

Ralph Waldo Emerson wrote, "Don't waste yourself in rejection, or bark against the bad." Still, rejection in all its forms can sting. You spent time and energy on an application; you may have pictured yourself enjoying your first year at a certain college. Life sometimes takes us in a surprising direction. Millionaire Bo Bennett points out that "rejection is nothing more than a necessary step in the pursuit of success."

Your rejection, whether from one school or from several, can feel crushing. Of course, it comes at a time when your friends and classmates are sharing their news. You may feel jealousy and

Waitlisted? An Action Plan

Odds of getting off a waiting list and into the college are not good. In 2008, the National Association for College Admission Counseling (NACAC) found that only 30 percent of students waitlisted were accepted in the end. Here are steps you can take if you are waitlisted:

1. Learn your options immediately. When will the school send its final decision? According to the NACAC, the college must notify you by August 1 at the latest.
2. Find out what financial aid will be available to you once the college has distributed funds to students accepted at the traditional time.
3. Hold a place at a school that accepted you. Do you need to send a deposit to secure a spot? (You might lose this money, but you'll find it's a small price to pay for peace of mind.)
4. Bring in the reinforcements. Do you know an alumnus of the college who would be willing to write a letter on your behalf? Some colleges will accept this, but contact the admissions department to ask permission first.
5. Send supplemental information or news of recent awards to better argue your case. You might want to consult with your high school counselor. Since there is an art to being persistent without being pushy, a counselor's advice will be helpful.

resentment toward others celebrating an acceptance. However, the decision does not end here for anyone. The students who were accepted will still need to look at finances. Those who were rejected will regroup and, if they are determined to, will create a successful next step.

However you grapple with the disappointment, remember that the rejection of your application is not personal. Despite the time and good intentions that a college puts into reading each application, it still doesn't make the right decision 100 percent of the time each year. If the rejection gnaws at you, consider calling the college's admissions department to gain some insight. They get these calls all the time, and if they can, they may give you some insight into their reasons for rejection. It may sting a little, but it may be constructive criticism. Hear them out and learn from it.

If you continue to feel that you belong at the school in question, you might consider appealing the decision. While highly selective colleges discourage appeals, other schools handle them in different, often surprising, ways. Maybe you have reviewed your application and found things missing. Maybe you have recent achievements, awards, or test scores that you want to advertise. An admissions dean tells *U.S. News and World Report* that they will consider appeals from persuasive students, but only if the persuasion comes directly from the student and not from his or her family. In other words, the school needs to see that you want admission and are willing to fight for it.

Beyond fighting for a spot now, you are always free to reapply in a semester or two. If you are certain you belong at that college, consider taking some community college classes and create some new credentials for yourself. You can also begin college at a different school and apply as a transfer student later. Or you might want to plan a work/gap year while you regroup for reapplication. A year may seem painfully long now, but if you want a degree from a particular college badly enough, you'll be glad you were persistent. In the meantime, compose a letter to the admission's department restating your interest in the school and announcing plans to reapply.

If the college has placed you on its waitlist, you may not be sure what to expect. To protect yourself, try to decide if the school is your first choice. If you are accepted, you may only have a short time to accept the offer. Check to see if the delay in acceptance will impact your access to housing and financial aid choices. If you call, the admissions staff may be able to tell you your "rank" on the list and whether or not they expect to have that many open spots in the freshman class (because of accepted students going elsewhere). This could indicate your chances of getting in and help you determine your next step.

Making Lemonade from Lemons: Regroup and Redefine Your Plan

Remember, if the application and acceptance process didn't go the way you'd hoped, you are not destined to float along on a second-rate future. Take your lemons and make lemonade. Give yourself time to emotionally detach from the colleges you'd dreamed about. Close your eyes and imagine yourself living your life after college. Where do you want to be in ten years? Is there another path to get you there? Many successful people have been rejected from prestigious colleges. Some built their careers starting with the most affordable option their families could manage and went on to lead ground-breaking lives.

Knowing yourself and your goals can help keep you centered during the college admissions process.

There is more than one college that will serve you well, introducing you to exciting classes, good friends, and fantastic memories. There is more than one road to get you there. As a high school senior, Meredith set her sights on a prestigious liberal arts college and applied under its early admission program, never dreaming that she was making the wrong choice for herself. The college pushed her into the general admission category. She was determined to get in. "I wanted to prove to them that they should love me and accept me into their institution. They did." But more than a year into her college program, she grew to regret her decision. In retrospect, she says, "I was in love with the idea" of the school, not the reality. "I think if I had taken more time to talk with students, look at the direction their broadcasting program takes a student, and thought more about what I wanted out of my life besides my job, I may have decided not to go [there]. But the future was too far away at that point. I was eighteen."

Meredith's transfer school is a small, Catholic, historically all-women's college near her hometown. She recognizes now that "I need to feel . . . like I am a part of their student body and I matter to them. It is a small, nurturing environment, which is just what I need at this point in my life." Years after you graduate college, your success will be driven more by your initiative and passion and less by the name on your degree.

A New Phase

As you complete your time in high school and prepare for the next step, new decisions will present themselves at every turn. If you will be living at college, can you choose your roommate? If you are requesting to live with a friend or acquaintance, are your personalities compatible? Finding a good match ensures a

When you move into a college dormitory, you enter into a brand-new chapter of your life. When talking with your new roommate, see how compatible you are when it comes to socializing, cleanliness, and more.

peaceful first year in which to grow and learn. What classes will you take and how will they help you explore your interests? How will you balance work, classes, and college life? If you will continue to live at home, how will you make extra time to stay on campus and meet new people? You will be surprised by the ways you answer these questions and begin growing into the person you will become.

acceptance The state of being accepted or admitted as a student to a college or training school.

admission The act of being allowed into a program of study at a college or training school. A college's admissions department handles and reviews all college applications.

allowance A sum of money granted for a specific purpose, such as personal or living expenses.

appeal To ask for support or aid, or to contest a decision like a college rejection.

associate's degree A degree given by a community college after one completes two years of full-time study or a longer period of part-time study.

autobiographical A way of writing or speaking that deals with one's life experience.

certificate A document that proves you have completed a course or program.

community college A public junior college with the purpose of serving college students in that community; also known as a two-year college.

defer To deliberately put off or delay.

disciplinary A type of action taken against a student in response to a violation of student rules.

early decision A college admission plan in which students apply earlier in the year than the typical application deadline and receive an acceptance/rejection notice earlier. Early decision usually requires that you agree to attend that college if admitted, though the conditions vary by college.

enrollment An official registration or entrance into an academic program.

financial aid Money given to a student enrolled in a college or other program. Aid can be qualified as need-based or non-need-based. Financial aid can come from the college itself, from a government program, or from another outside source. Loans, grants, and scholarships are all considered financial aid.

gap year   A period of time between high school graduation and enrollment in college that a student chooses to spend in some other pursuit. Usually, this time is created by deferring official enrollment in a college. Gap year activities can include service work, internships, traditional work for pay, and travel.

internship   An official or unofficial training program that provides a student or young person with practical experience in a job. An internship may be paid or unpaid.

liberal arts   A course of study containing an overview of knowledge that includes writing, language, critical thought, math, science, and the arts.

major   An academic study or interest upon which a student focuses his or her program and, as a result, becomes more skilled and informed.

merit-based   Based on personal achievement or personal qualities, regardless of financial need.

need-based   Based on financial need.

philosophy   A collection of principles that guide an organization or person. A college's philosophy reflects its beliefs about its students and how they should learn.

semester   A division in the academic year that usually lasts between fifteen and eighteen weeks and contains a planned schedule of classes.

stipend   A payment, sometimes in the form of a scholarship or allowance, to a student.

study abroad A course of study done in a foreign country, usually during college. The academic credit from studying abroad can be credited toward your college degree.

technical A type of education or training that can be vocational (teaching a specific trade) or science-specific. Technical colleges offer degrees in scientific programs and may also offer certificate programs in a number of areas: IT, design, medical fields, mechanics, and more.

transcript An official report from a previously attended school (such as high school or another college) that includes classes taken and grades received.

undergraduate Refers to the degree program leading to a bachelor's degree. Students in a bachelor's program are also referred to as undergraduates.

U.S. Census An official review of the U.S. population that includes details about individuals, including age, ethnicity, living conditions, family structure, income, education, etc. The Census is taken every ten years.

violation An act that breaks a rule or law.

virtual tour An online, visual introduction to a place like a college campus or a town.

vocational Related to a career. A vocational school or college program seeks to train its students in a specific job-related skill.

waitlist Shortened phrase that refers to a waiting list. Students waitlisted by a college are not officially accepted until the college knows how many accepted students will enroll, and how many will decline.

Association of Canadian Community Colleges
1223 Michael Street North, Suite 200
Ottawa, ON K1J 7T2
Canada
(613) 746-2222
Web site: http://www.accc.ca
The national organization of Canadian community colleges, this
association's site contains a full list of member colleges and
a searchable database of programs. Information is available
in both English and French.

Campus Starter
210-4475 Viewmont Avenue
Victoria, BC V8Z 6L8
Canada
(250) 708-0022
Web site: http//www.campusstarter.com
Owned by the EI Group, which also publishes *Campus Starter*
magazine, this site organizes Canadian colleges and their
academic programs for comparison. Students can also take
virtual tours of the campuses and engage in online forums.

College Board
45 Columbus Avenue
New York, NY 10023-6917
(866) 630-9305
Web site: http://www.collegeboard.com
A nonprofit association of colleges, the College Board provides
an online clearinghouse of information that advises on everything from college test prep to finding financial aid. The Web
site allows you to store and change favorite colleges.

Corporation for National and Community Service
1201 New York Avenue NW
Washington, DC 20525
(202) 606-5000
Web site: http://www.nationalservice.gov
This organization funds the AmeriCorps program and other
service work opportunities, with educational benefits for
participants of some programs.

Education Resources Institute (TERI)
Park Square Building
31 St. James, Suite 950
Boston, MA 02116
(800) 255-8374
Web site: http://www.teri.org
This nonprofit organization helps underserved, first-generation,
minority, and low-income students navigate the college
application and financial aid processes.

National Survey on Student Engagement
Indiana University Center for Postsecondary Research
1900 East Tenth Street, Suite 419
Bloomington, IN 47406
(812) 856-5824
Web site: http://www.nsse.iub.edu
A free copy of a survey that measures the satisfaction of college
students nationwide is available online.

Peterson's
Princeton Pike Corporate Center
2000 Lenox Drive

Lawrenceville, NJ 08648

(609) 896-1800

Web site: http://www.petersons.com

Peterson's publishes books, Web sites, and other materials for
the college application market and for various educational
and youth employment opportunities. The site provides
searchable college and program databases and a "My
Peterson's" feature in which to organize college information,
application deadlines, scholarships, test prep tools, and
online forums.

ReadySetLaunch

Yale University

P.O. Box 206484

New Haven, CT 06520

Web site: http://www.readysetlaunch.org

ReadySetLaunch is a nonprofit organization that seeks to match
high-achieving, low-income students with free college application consulting by pairing them with an Ivy League college
student. High school students apply and are matched with a
mentor in the spring of their junior year, and mentoring con-
tinues throughout the entire college application process.

Web Sites

Due to the changing nature of Internet links, Rosen Publishing
has developed an online list of Web sites related to the subject
of this book. This site is updated regularly. Please use this link
to access this list:

http://www.rosenlinks.com/col/mrcc

Benvenuto, Mark. *College Prowler, Big Book of Colleges, 2009*. Pittsburgh, PA: College Prowler, 2008.

College Board. *Book of Majors, 2008*. New York, NY: College Board, 2008.

College Board. *International Student Handbook, 2009* (International Student Handbook of U.S. Colleges). New York, NY: College Board, 2008.

Csikszentmihalyi, Mihaly. *Flow: The Psychology of Optimal Experience*. New York, NY: Harper Perennial, 2008.

Dabbah, Mariela. *Latinos in College: Your Guide to Success*. Briarcliff Manor, NY: Consultare, 2009.

Doe, Mimi, and Michele A. Hernandez. *Don't Worry, You'll Get In: 100 Winning Tips for Stress-Free College Admissions*. Cambridge, MA: Da Capo Press, 2005.

Ehrenhaft, George. *Writing a Successful College Essay*. 4th ed. Hauppauge, NY: Barron's Educational Series, Inc., 2008.

Fiske, Edward. *Fiske Guide to Colleges, 2009*. Naperville, IL: Sourcebooks, Inc., 2008.

Hernandez, Michele A. *Acing the College Application: How to Maximize Your Chances for Admission to the College of Your Choice*. New York, NY: Ballantine Books, 2007.

Hughes, Chuck. *What It Really Takes to Get into Ivy League and Other Highly Selective Colleges*. New York, NY: McGraw-Hill, 2003.

Jager-Hyman, Joie. *Fat Envelope Frenzy: One Year, Five Promising Students, and the Pursuit of the Ivy League Prize*. New York, NY: Harper, 2008.

Landes, Michael. *The Back Door Guide to Short-Term Job Adventures: Internships, Summer Jobs, Seasonal Work, Volunteer Vacations, and Transitions Abroad*. 4th ed. Berkeley, CA: Ten Speed Press, 2005.

London, Michael. *The New Rules of College Admissions: Ten Former Admissions Officers Reveal What It Takes to Get into College Today*. New York, NY: Fireside Books, 2006.

O'Shaughnessy, Lynn. *The College Solution: A Guide for Everyone Looking for the Right School at the Right Price*. Upper Saddle River, NJ: FT Press, 2008.

Page, Cristina. *The Smart Girl's Guide to College: A Serious Book Written by Women in College to Help You*. New York, NY: Noonday Press, 1997.

Peterson's. *Two-Year Colleges, 2009* (Peterson's Two-Year Colleges). Lawrenceville, NJ: Peterson's, 2008.

Spring, Sally P., and Marion R. Franck. *Admission Matters: What Students and Parents Need to Know About Getting into College* (Jossey Bass Education Series). Hoboken, NJ: Jossey-Bass, 2005.

U.S. News Ultimate College Guide 2009. Naperville, IL: Sourcebooks, Inc., 2008.

Valverde, Leonard A. *The Latino Student's Guide to College Success*. Westport, CT: Greenwood Press, 2008.

Arenson, Karen W. "Applications to Colleges Are Breaking Records." *New York Times*, January 17, 2008. Retrieved March 2009 (http://www.nytimes.com/2008/01/17/education/17admissions.html).

Clark, Kim. "Four Reasons a Rejection Letter Isn't Always the End." *U.S. News and World Report*, March 10, 2009. Retrieved March 2009 (http://www.usnews.com/articles/education/2009/10/4-reasons-a-rejection-letter-isnt-always-the-end.html).

Coetzee, Melinda. "Investigating the Impact of "the Gap Year" on Career Decision-Making." Master's thesis, University of Pretoria, South Africa, 2006.

CollegeBoard.com. "Community College: Myth vs. Reality." Retrieved March 2009 (http://www.collegeboard.com/student/csearch/where-to-start/150494.html).

Constant, Meredith. E-mail interview with author, March 2009.

Crawford, Matthew B. "The Case for Working with Your Hands," *New York Times*, May 21, 2009. Retrieved June 2009 (http://www.nytimes.com/2009/05/24/magazine/24labor-t.html).

Ducey, Charles, William Fitzsimmons, and Marlyn E. McGrath. "Time Out or Burnout for the Next Generation." Harvard University, 2006. Retrieved March 2009 (http://www.admissions.college.harvard.edu/apply/time_off/index.html).

Ehrenhaft, George. *Writing a Successful College Essay*. 4th ed. Hauppauge, NY: Barron's Educational Series, Inc., 2008

Flowers, Lamont A., Lawrence Flowers, and James L. Moore. "African American Students' Satisfaction with Distance Education Courses." StudentAffairs.com, Winter 2008. Retrieved March 2009 (http://studentaffairs.com/ejournal/Winter_2008/AfricanAmericanStudents.html).

Gustavson, Adam. Interview with author, April 2009.

Hernandez, Michele A. *Acing the College Application: How to Maximize Your Chances for Admission to the College of Your Choice*. New York, NY: Ballantine Books, 2007.

Kelley, Rob."College Grades See Big Income Boost." CNN Money, October 26, 2006. Retrieved March 2009 (http://money.cnn.com/2006/10/25/pf/college/census_degree/index.htm).

Mallon, Andrea. E-mail interview with author, March 2009.

Miro, Theresa. E-mail interview with author, March 2009.

National Center for Fair and Open Testing. "10 Myths About the SAT." August 20, 2007. Retrieved June 2009 (http://www.fairtest.org/10-myths-about-sat).

O'Connell, Martha. "How to Choose a College That's Right for You." National Public Radio, February 21, 2007.

Old Dominion University. "Is Distance Learning for Me?" Student Questionnaire, 2004. Retrieved March 2009 (http://www.clt.odu.edu/oso/index.php?src=pe_isdlforme_info).

Silva, Marney. E-mail interview with author, March 2009.

Sloan Consortium, "Making the Grade: Online Education in the United States, 2006." November 9, 2006. Retrieved March 2009 (http://www.sloanconsortium.org/publications/survey/survey06.asp).

Smith, Anne Kates. "Checking Out Colleges Without the Trip." *Kiplinger's Personal Finance*, April 5, 2009, pp. G03.

U.S. Department of Education National Center for Education Statistics. "National Postsecondary Student Aid Study." 1995–1996. Retrieved March 2009 (http://nces.ed.gov/NPSAS).

U.S. Department of Labor. "Futurework: Trends and Challenges for Work in the 21st Century." September 1999. Retrieved March 2009 (http://www.dol.gov/oasam/programs/history/herman/reports/futurework/report.htm).

About the Author

Annalise Silivanch is area chair of communications at the University of Phoenix in Jersey City, New Jersey. Her college instruction experience includes teaching writing, research, and public speaking, as well as coaching students to set personal and professional goals for themselves.

Photo Credits

Cover, p. 1 © www.istockphoto.com/Andrew Rich; pp. 5, 32–33 © David Young-Wolff/Photo Edit; p. 7 © John Giustina/Getty Images; p. 8 © www.istockphoto.com; pp. 10, 23, 29, 41, 49, 54, 59, 61© www.istockphoto.com/Robert Dant; pp. 11, 53 © Shutterstock; pp. 15 © Bill Bachman/Photo Edit; p. 17 © www.istockphoto.com/Lisa F. Young; p. 18 © Rudi Von Briel/Photo Edit; pp. 20–21 © Tony Savino/The Image Works; pp. 31, 50–51 © Newscom; p. 35 © West Rock/Getty Images; p. 36 © Kate M. Deloma/Photo Edit; p. 43 © www.istockphoto.com/Loretta Hostettler; p. 58 © Colin Young-Wolff/Photo Edit; p. 60 © Ken Reed/Getty Images; p. 64 © www.istockphoto.com/Jason Stitt; p. 66 © Cindy Charles/Photo Edit.

Designer: Nicole Russo; Editor: Andrea Sclarow; Photo Researcher: Marty Levick